Hailes Abbey

GLOUCESTERSHIRE

J G COAD MA, FSA

Inspector of Ancient Monuments and Historic Buildings

Richard, Earl of Cornwall, was in grave danger at sea in October 1242. He vowed that if he lived he would found a religious house. In 1245 his brother, King Henry III, gave him the manor of Hailes so that he could keep his pledge.

After its establishment, Richard's son, Edmund, presented the Cistercian monks of Hailes Abbey with a phial said to contain the blood of Christ. From then until the Dissolution, Hailes became a magnet for pilgrims.

This handbook will help you understand the interesting and extensive ruins and the history of the abbey. The excellent museum contains a variety of exhibits on the history of Hailes, both as a monastic site and as a post-Dissolution home.

ENGLISH HERITAGE · LONDON

Contents

Published by English Heritage
23 Savile Row, London W1X 2HE
© Copyright English Heritage 1970
Previously published by HMSO 1982
First published by English Heritage 1985. Second edition 1993, reprinted 1995, 1997, 1999
Printed in England for Tactica Solutions
Dd.004013243 05/99 C60 matrix 076368 FA5634.
ISBN 1 85074 466 1

Descriptive Tour

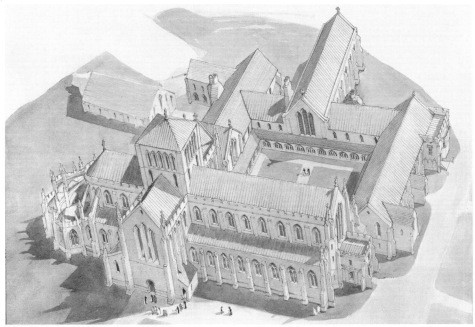

Hailes Abbey as it may have appeared in the late fifteenth century   TERRY BALL

The plan on page 4 will help you follow your tour and understand the description of the abbey as it is and as it was built. The Glossary at the back of the book should be referred to for an explanation of technical terms.

After leaving the ticket office and museum, the site of the abbey church is to the left of the ruins in front of you (see the plan and the aerial view on page 5).

ABBEY CHURCH

Although little remains above ground now, the excavations at the beginning of this century revealed the complete plan of the church. This shows it to have been in its later form a building some 341ft (104m) in length, with a nave width of 63ft (19m). It was built of Cotswold stone, quarried locally, with details in blue lias.

As completed in the mid 1250s, the layout followed contemporary Cistercian practice. The nave was of eight bays approached from the west through double doors, flanked by three orders of shafts having bases of blue lias. Outside the west end was a small porch. No trace of this remains above ground. Possibly it was a contraction of an earlier Galilee, such as survives at Fountains Abbey, but this is by no means certain. Flanking the nave were side aisles, the third and fourth bays of which were apparently converted

3

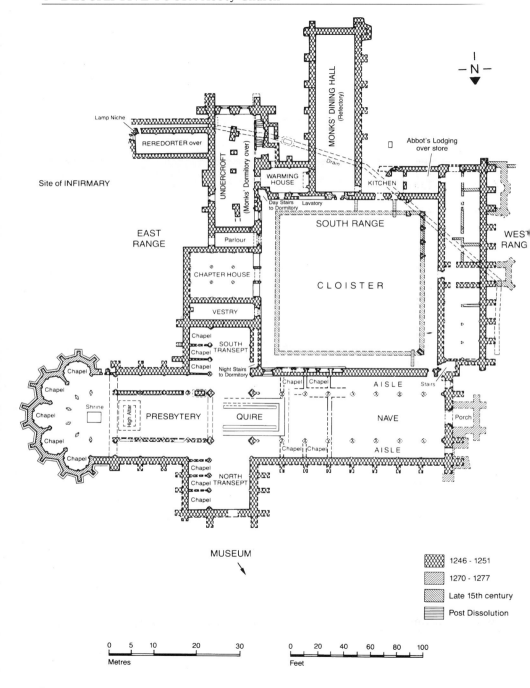

MUSEUM

▨	1246 - 1251
▨	1270 - 1277
▨	Late 15th century
▤	Post Dissolution

The rounded east end of the church can be seen at the top of this aerial view, the square cloister garth is in the centre and the monks' dining hall is to the right. The ticket office and museum are at the far left

into chapels, possibly in the fourteenth century. In the westernmost bay of the south side is the base of the lay brothers' night stairs, and adjacent to it, to the east, was the second processional door to the cloister. At the east end of the south aisle is the other entrance to the cloister.

The internal arrangements were of the conventional Cistercian kind. The five western bays of the nave formed the lay brothers' quire, with its own altar at the eastern end. To the east, a single screened bay formed the retro-quire for aged and ill monks, and beyond this was the pulpitum leading to the monks' quire which extended under the crossing and almost to the presbytery steps.

North and south of the crossing of the church, which probably had a short tower over it, were four bay transepts, each having three eastern chapels,

separated from each other by stone partitions. When originally excavated, evidence for a doorway was found in the north wall of the north transept. Possibly this formed a pilgrims' entrance in addition to its main function of providing access to the monks' cemetery. In the south wall of the south transept was a doorway leading to the vestry; the width of the west wall here is evidence that the night stairs from the monks' dormitory (dorter) were contained within the thickness, emerging to the south of the northwest angle shaft of the transept. This latter feature clearly derives from the plan of Beaulieu (see page 18).

The original presbytery was of four bays, flanked by side aisles approached up two steps from the crossing. It terminated at the high altar, traces of which still remain, and behind this was the main east wall. Although the latter was entirely demolished in the rebuilding of the 1270s, its position has been marked out in the turf. Flanking it were twin turrets, both containing spiral stairs. Part of the south one is visible.

In the westernmost bay of the south aisle of the presbytery was a small lavatorium, with its drain running westwards beside the crossing pier; a similar arrangement to those at Jervaulx and Roche. In the third bay on the same side, the thickening of the screen wall indicates the position of the piscina and sedilia. As with the nave floor, the presbytery was covered with glazed tiles, many of them bearing the eagle of Richard, Earl of Cornwall, and the paly for Sanchia of Provence, his second wife.

When in 1270 Edmund presented to Hailes a phial of the "holy blood," this was placed with due ceremony in a shrine especially built for it. It seems probable that this shrine had two positions, the earlier one being only a temporary one, and as yet unidentified positively. For such a worthy relic, a dignified setting within the church was an obvious requirement. As its arrival seems to have coincided with a serious fire in the monastery, the decision was taken to extend the east end by one bay and throw out a ring, or chevet of chapels. This design allowed space for a processional aisle in front of these, and in the centre, behind the high altar, a suitably focal space for the shrine. The rebuilding of the east end took six years to complete, and the lower courses can be seen today. As with the rest of the church, the chapels were vaulted; some of the bases for the wall shafts still survive. To the west of the southernmost chapel was a doorway leading to the infirmary.

The foundations of the shrine are still there, and show it to have been a structure some 10ft (3m) in length by 8ft 6in (2.6m) wide. It is set in a slightly off-centre position, suggesting that the

The east end of the abbey church. See also the reconstruction illustrations on pages 3 and 19

Three of five arched recesses in the north wall of the cloister. These date from the original construction of the abbey and were probably used as book cupboards

foundations for it were put in before the original east end of the church was demolished. The footings give an indication of the size. It is unfortunate that nothing remains to show what form the structure took above, but it may have been comparable to the surviving shrine of Edward the Confessor in Westminster Abbey.

CLOISTER

In a Cistercian community, provision had to be made not only for the monks but also for the *conversi* (lay brothers). In practice this meant that the monks had the east and south sides of the cloister, the lay brothers the west. To save space, it was usual for the monks' refectory (see page 14) to be sited at right angles to the south range, instead of parallel to it as in other Orders.

What form the original cloister at Hailes took is not absolutely certain, as in the fifteenth century, probably under Abbot Whitchurch, it was entirely rebuilt. Judging by the coats-of-arms carved on the vaulting bosses, now in the museum, alterations to the cloister were going on almost until the Dissolution in 1539.

Recent excavation suggests that the early cloister was a simple wooden pentice structure; three surviving corbels towards the south end of the east range support this view.

Along the north side are the remains of a stone bench, and built into the church wall are five arched recesses, the three to the west being the best preserved (see above). As at Beaulieu these were to disguise buttresses strengthening the south aisle wall. The recesses date from the original construction of the abbey and probably were used as book cupboards. When the vaulting was

> BONUM EST NOS HIC ESSE, QUIA HOMO VIVIT PURIUS,
> CADIT RARIUS, SURGIT VELOCIUS, INCEDIT CAUTIUS,
> QUIESCIT SECURIUS, MORITUR FELICIUS,
> PURGATUR CITIUS, PRÆMIATUR COPIOSIUS;
> SAINT BERNARD.

It is good to be here. Here man more purely lives, less oft doth fall, more promptly rises, walks with stricter heed, more safely rests, dies happier, is freed earlier from cleansing fires, and gains withall a brighter crown [quotation on the north wall of the cloister]

Hailes Abbey in 1732, from an engraving by Samuel and Nathaniel Buck

inserted in the fifteenth century, it was fitted in with little regard for earlier work, as is very evident here and on the east range. The corbels to carry the vaulting ribs were carved in the shape of angels, each carrying a shield. One is on display in the museum cloister, and two more remain *in situ* set above the book cupboards.

In the second arched recess from the west there is a change in the colour of the sandstone, that to the west being a deeper yellow. This may mark a break in the construction of the original church, which would have been built from east to west. It is possible that building work stopped here once the quire had been completed and was only resumed after the principal buildings of the first cloister had been finished.

The inner walls of the cloister survive for the most part at foundation level, although at the south end of the west range three bays of the late fifteenth-century rebuilding stand to their full height. In the central bay some of the perpendicular tracery survives with its trefoil heads.

In its final form the cloister was ten bays square. The inner foundations,

although not visible, have external buttresses and internal projections to carry the bases of the vaulting shafts. In front of the chapter house doorway two extra large buttresses were found, which suggest an elaborate porch leading into the garth. This had been blocked at some stage by the insertion of a rough stone wall. To the west of the refectory doorway in the south range the various foundations projecting into the cloister represent post-Dissolution alterations.

It was customary for Cistercian abbeys to make separate provision for the lay brothers on the west side of the cloister. Here they had their own walk between the west walk of the monks and the east wall of the west range. If such an arrangement existed at Hailes, it was swept away in the fifteenth-century rebuilding. At this time the abbots appropriated the west range for their own use and the Bucks' view shown above suggests the final form which this range took before the Dissolution in 1536.

EAST RANGE
This follows conventional Cistercian

The arch on the left is the doorway to the chapter house, the third arch leads to the parlour and the fourth to the undercroft of the dormitory (dorter). On the right are the day stairs to the dormitory

practice; next to the south transept was the vestry, then the chapter house, parlour and dormitory undercroft with dormitory above.

Vestry

The vestry formed a long narrow chamber, some 12ft 6in (3.8m) wide, running the full length of the south wall of the south transept, and connecting with the latter by a doorway almost midway along the wall (see the plan). It was vaulted in three bays, two attached shafts with deep roll mouldings partly surviving at the west end, with the badly eroded base of a shaft a third of the way along the south wall.

The vestry was approached from the cloister by a handsome double doorway, the door being set behind two trefoil-headed openings which in turn were carried on a central shaft, the base for which still survives. Above was a quatrefoil window with deep roll moulding, the upper sections of which still remain. In the jambs below can be seen the remains of barholes for securing the door.

When the cloister was reconstructed late in the fifteenth century, and a vaulted roof inserted, the upper portion of the doorway was hacked back to accommodate the new design. The new arrangement can be more clearly seen in the parlour doorway.

Chapter house

Adjoining the vestry to the south lay the chapter house (see the illustration on page 20). After the church, this formed a central part of the life of a Cistercian monastery. The monks gathered in here to listen to a chapter from the Rule of St Benedict every day, and the richness of the decoration here is an indication of the importance of this room in the life of the community.

The Hailes chapter house was square ended, as was usual in Cistercian abbeys, and vaulted in three bays and three spans. Two attached vaulting shafts remain at the west end, as do the moulded quatrefoil bases for the four columns. At the east end, resited, is the stump of a triple attached vaulting shaft. Some of the wall seating remains towards the cloister end.

In the museum some of the vaulting bosses can be seen. These still have traces of red paint on them; when they were first excavated there were also remains of gilding. These, combined with the blue lias shafting and stained glass, show that the monks of Hailes had no lack of colour in their daily lives.

The chapter house was entered from the cloister through double doors set in a finely moulded archway. The hood moulding of this doorway is of later date than those above the adjacent arches, and probably dates from a partial reconstruction in the 1270s. On the south side of the doorway remains the fragmentary base of a detached shaft. Flanking the doorway are two arches, the triple moulding of which has been badly damaged, as have the sills. None of the tracery or jamb shafts from these windows survives, though below the southern end of the south arch can be seen a base for a detached shaft which once connected with the arch above.

Parlour

South of the chapter house lay the parlour, a narrow room, open at both ends and providing access from the cloister to the infirmary passage. Only in this room was conversation allowed, silence being the rule in the rest of the

Looking east across the cloister from the west range. The three arches on the left are the only three remaining window arches of the cloister walk; the central arch on the other side of the cloister garth is the doorway to the chapter house

monastic buildings.

The remains of stone benches can be seen at the western end on both sides. The doorway from the cloister exhibits three periods of building. The earliest, dating from the foundation of the abbey, is represented by the semi-circular moulded label on the western face; below it, and more easily seen from the east, is an interesting cinquefoil-headed door-way, an insertion of the late thirteenth century.

In the fifteenth century, probably during the period of cloister rebuilding, a segmental arch was inserted springing from the original jamb-shafts. In this is the setting for a later corbel inserted to carry the cloister vaulting.

Dormitory (dorter) and undercroft

Above the east range was the monks' dormitory. No trace of this survives, but a considerable amount of the undercroft does. This was an impressive room of six bays, vaulted in two spans with a line of pillars down the centre, a total of 89ft (27.1m) in length. At the south end the corners were strengthened with four large buttresses, some of the plinths of which survive. The undercroft was lit from this end by two windows, one to each bay. Only the lower part of the splays remains, together with the sills.

The undercroft was entered from the cloister through a doorway having a semi-circular hoodmould (the last doorway before the daystairs). The base of a detached shaft can be seen on the north side (on your right after passing through the doorway). Inside, the doorway was strengthened at a later date by an inserted splay.

In the third and sixth bays on the east side are hearths, the southern one of which had substantial traces of the coursed stone fireback remaining. The second bay on the east side has remains

of a doorway, probably leading to the infirmary court. From the fifth bay projects the undercroft to the reredorter (latrines).

On the west side the second bay contains a double cupboard, rebated for doors and grooved for shelves. The adjoining bay to the south contains a doorway giving access to the warming house; this is a later insertion, partly blocked. Between here and the south end there has been much alteration, most of it probably post-Dissolution. This accounts for the various later walls immediately to the west of the undercroft.

Between the fourth and sixth bays on the west the main wall thickens to accommodate a small double-sided latrine. Entrance to this was gained from the undercroft through two doors; traces of the reveals of these can be seen at the south end adjoining the southwestern vaulting shaft base and in the fourth bay. Short flights of steps led down to the latrine which connects with the main drain immediately below. In the wall to the west of the southern flight of steps are the remains of a water chute. This probably led to a small hand-basin before discharging into the main drain through a small hole in the floor.

Latrines (reredorter)

The monks' latrines were in a building of four bays running east from the monks' dorter. They were carried on a vaulted undercroft, to the south of which was the main drain of the abbey. This drain, a considerable constructional feat, is flushed from further up the hill and runs under part of the south range, the cloister garth and lay brothers' range, where it serves their own reredorter, before emerging to the west of the abbey. It is stone-vaulted throughout, and is joined by a second drain of similar size in the field to the west. This one runs off in a southerly direction. It and its associated buildings have yet to be investigated.

The first floor of the reredorter has gone completely, but the undercroft still contains features of interest. In the north wall is a large semi-circular fireplace with a tiled hearth and the base of a pillar for carrying the hood. This wall appears to have been strengthened by a single buttress; internally, all trace of the vaulting shafts has gone. The south wall has three of its attached shafts relatively complete; at the west end the base of one survives, and between the third and fourth bay can be seen marks on the wall where the shaft from here was hacked off.

No trace of any access to this undercroft was found except at the east end. Here, in the southern corner, stairs led up to the first floor. To the side a well-made lamp niche can be seen, the interior of which has a dome and small flue. At a later date, the line of the stairs was altered and the level of the lower steps raised. In this form they led to an inward-opening doorway. The purpose of this alteration is uncertain. To the left of the stairs a blocked doorway can be seen, with the remains of a chamfered reveal on its south side. At the east end of the south wall is a doorway, rebated on the inside, leading to a small garderobe that discharged into the main drain below. Immediately to the west of this doorway are traces of a wall cupboard, with rebate for a wooden frame and door.

SOUTH RANGE

The south and west ranges were considerably altered in the sixteenth and seventeenth centuries when they were adapted for domestic purposes. They were largely demolished in the eighteenth century.

Following Cistercian practice the south range contained the warming house, the monks' refectory, running at right angles to the cloister, and the kitchen. At the east end can be seen the beginning of the day stairs leading to the dorter.

Warming house

This is to the west of the day stairs. It was the only place apart from the kitchen and the infirmary where rules of the Order allowed a fire. Originally entered through a round-headed doorway, the remains of which can be seen above the trefoil-headed insertion of the 1270s, this was a room of two vaulted bays.

In the west wall are the remains of a large segmental-backed fireplace some 9ft (2.7m) wide. At the north end of this survive the first floor courses of the moulded jamb which carried the fireplace hood. In the opposite, east, wall there was originally a large cupboard extending almost the full width of the room under the arch of the day stairs. This had a wooden front, the rebate for the frame being visible at its north side and adjacent to the southeast angle pillar. Originally, this cupboard appears to have been raised on a stone base standing some 12 to 15in (30 to 38cm) above the warming house floor, the front of the base being finished with a wooden sill beam, the sockets for which are visible. The cupboard was lit by a small internally shuttered window in the south wall.

After the Dissolution, an entrance was cut through to the adjacent dorter undercroft and the stone base removed. This entrance has been partly blocked. In the western half of the north wall are the remains of a large double-headed cupboard, originally divided by a mullion. Traces of a rebate survive in the bottom right corner. Most of the north wall has been extensively altered; however, part of the attached vaulting shafts and springers survives from the original building of 1250. The south wall has likewise been much altered.

Lavatory

In the cloister, between the warming house and the refectory door, was the monks' lavatory (washing place). The present one dates from the fifteenth century and consists of a segmental arch 18ft 6in (5.6m) wide, with trefoil-ended panels in the soffit. It is recessed into the walls of both warming house and refectory. At its east end can be seen the semicircular groove which once held the end of a long stone basin. This would have been supplied from a row of taps above. The drain from it ran under the refectory to the main culvert.

To the left of the centre of the arch are the remains of a corbel for the cloister vaulting. Behind the arch can be seen traces of the earlier lavatory, a considerably taller structure.

Dining hall (refectory)

As with most of the southern range, this has suffered considerably from post-Dissolution alterations. It was a long building and was supported by substantial buttresses; it measures 116 by 30ft (35 by 9m).

The refectory (see the reconstruction illustration on page 14) would have had a high timber roof, possibly supported by a row of pillars in the centre. The Bucks' view of 1732 (see page 8) shows it as having been lit at the north end by tall lancet windows.

The refectory was approached from the cloister through a richly moulded doorway having two free shafts of blue lias between three engaged ones of oolite. These supported capitals of lias which had elaborately undercut stiff-leaf foliage. Apart from the lias shafts, the west jamb is reasonably complete, though badly worn. The eastern one has been extensively cut away, most likely in

North end of the dining hall (refectory). Compare this with the reconstruction illustration on page 14

TERRY BALL

The abbot and his guests sat on a dais at the south end of the dining hall. On the left was a pulpit from which readings were given while the monks ate. Food was served from the centre of the room; spoons, bowls and napkins were kept in the cupboards in the far wall

connection with the alterations to the lavatory. Probably at the same time during the fifteenth century the original doorway was partly infilled and the present narrower doorway inserted.

To the east of this doorway a crude squint can be seen, and within survive the draw-bar holes. In this filling, on the inside, can be seen a twelfth-century capital, possibly from the parish church or castle.

The interior of the main north doorway has been as extensively altered as its exterior. On the west side, the base, part of the shaft and the capital of the original doorway survive, as does part of the richly moulded archway above. The east half had been rebuilt, possibly in the

fifteenth century, for there was apparently a serious fire in the refectory then.

Partly obscured by this rebuild is a trefoil-headed basin set into the wall. Although little trace remains of the basin, part of the drain survives; water was supplied from the same pipe that fed the lavatory on the other side of the wall. East of the basin are four trefoil-headed cupboards carved from a single block of stone and set below a segmental relieving arch. These must have once contained the community's few articles of cutlery. The western cupboard has a groove for a shelf, and its west end has been damaged at some period. The two eastern openings formed a double recess. Below them is a small cupboard with rebated jambs. Underneath it appears to run the drain from the lavatory; possibly the cupboard formed an inspection hatch. In the angle of the northeast corner of the refectory is the remains of another small basin.

To the west of the refectory doorway are two deep cupboards, rebated for doors, the iron pins for which still survive. Within them is a groove for a shelf. In the adjacent west wall is a doorway leading to the kitchen. The foundations of a cross-wall visible approximately halfway along the refectory are probably a post-Dissolution alteration. It is possible though that this wall represents a shortening of the refectory in the fifteenth century when the smaller community would not have needed such a large room. The stone drain in the middle of the room is a post-Dissolution insertion.

The raised floor at the south end of the refectory shows the position of the high table. The block of stone against the centre of the south wall may have been the base for a crucifix behind the abbot's chair. Seating for the monks was along the walls, which probably accounts for the ashlar not continuing to ground level. The gap in the west wall, with the irregular spacing of the buttresses here, probably indicates the site of the pulpitum and its stair.

Kitchen

This was to the west of the refectory, and supplied monks and lay brothers. This building was much altered in its later years, the Bucks' view showing it with a blocked first-floor door opening into the refectory and its north wall extending into the cloister. Very little pre-Dissolution work now survives, apart from the base of the north wall. The doorway to the cloister is a later insertion as is the cobbled area to the south.

Northwest of this cobbling is what appears at first sight to be the base of a buttress. But the chamfer on its northeast edge and traces of fire indicate that it was probably the base of one side of a huge open hearth extending along much of the south side of the kitchen.

West of the kitchen are three small rooms and a passage connecting with the south end of the west range. Originally, these were probably storerooms and food preparation rooms, while the passage was also used to carry food from the kitchen to the lay brothers' refectory.

WEST RANGE

In a Cistercian abbey such as Hailes, the west range originally provided a home for the lay brothers as well as storage space for the cellarer or storekeeper. Later, when the lay brothers had died out, abbots tended to appropriate an increasing amount of the range for their own use and by the time of the Dissolution west ranges were often houses of considerable splendour. Hailes appears to have been no exception to this worldly trend and after the Dissolution the abbot's house became the home of the Tracys. A similar progression accounts for the survival today of the abbot's house at Battle Abbey in Sussex, but at Hailes the house was ruinous by the end of the eighteenth century.

As originally laid out, the west range formed two substantial vaulted ground-floor rooms separated by a passage or parlour leading from the cloister to the outer court. This parlour was as far as visitors to the monks were allowed. The southern room was five bays long and originally was lit at its south end by two triple-light windows. This was the lay brothers' refectory or dining room, the raised floor level visible to the south end suggesting the position of the high table and implying a hierarchy similar to that in the monks' refectory. The blockings visible between the pillars are later insertions forming a series of small storerooms, probably built when the abbots were appropriating the range for their own use. Projecting west from the south end are two walls, all that remains of the tower visible in the Lysons's view on page 23. This tower is probably a late fifteenth-century addition to provide stairs to a presumed first-floor hall converted from the lay brothers' dormitory.

Projecting from the northwest corner of the former refectory is the base of a spiral staircase which once led up to the dormitory above. The shaft next to it, connecting with the main drain, may be all that remains of an indoor lavatory or washing place for the lay brothers. Later, it was converted to a latrine for the abbot's house. In the east end of the north wall steps lead up to a doorway to the central passage.

The central passage which linked the enclosed cloister with the busy outer court has been fairly extensively altered. Originally, the seclusion of the cloister was preserved by an inner and outer set of doors as can be seen by the surviving bases of the jambs. In common with the rooms on both sides, this passage was once vaulted. At its west end a porch projected into the outer court. Traces of a stone bench can be seen inside the south wall of the porch. The blue lias paving stones are a post-Dissolution alteration. At the east end of the north wall of the passage is a blocked doorway leading to the northern part of the west range.

The ground-floor room at the northern end was once a storeroom. Projecting from the northern end of the west wall is the base of the lay brothers' reredorter or latrine block, its position indicating that their dormitory once extended the full length of the first floor. The Kip view (page 25) shows what appears to be a projecting chapel for the abbot on the site of the reredorter. The stone coffin in the floor at the south end of the room was inserted after the Dissolution and its drain hole linked to the main drain, turning it into a doubtless effective if somewhat macabre sink.

History

A stream was diverted to bring water to the abbey and to fill its fish ponds. A further diversion was made to provide a flow to flush out the latrines

The Abbey of Hailes was one of the last Cistercian houses to be founded in England, some 118 years after the Order first established itself at Waverley in Surrey. The Cistercians were one of a number of Orders which grew up in the late eleventh and early twelfth century and which sought to re-create the more austere forms of religious life. Of these reformed Orders, the Cistercians and the ultra-strict Carthusians were the most successful. The Cistercians, founded in 1098 at the Burgundian abbey of Citeaux, sought to balance liturgical duties by an emphasis on manual labour; this took the form of agricultural work, much being done by a comparatively recent class of monks, the lay brothers (see Glossary). These often spent short

periods of time away from the monastery, living and working in the outlying parts of the estates in granges or farms. Discipline and uniformity of worship were ensured by visitations by the abbots of each community. To emphasise the self-sufficient and enclosed life of the Order, communities were sited in remote and lonely places.

Hailes was founded as the result of a vow made by Richard, Earl of Cornwall and King of the Romans, when he was in grave danger at sea in October 1242. Three years after this incident, Earl Richard's brother, King Henry III, granted to him the manor of Hailes to provide land for the fulfilment of this vow. Then, as now, Hailes was a small settlement occupying a secluded position near the foot of a westward-facing slope of the Cotswolds. The only other building of note seems to have been a castle, of which little is known. However, the nearby parish church is older than the abbey.

To provide the nucleus of a monastic community, Jordan, prior of the Cistercian abbey of Beaulieu in Hampshire, twenty monks and ten lay brothers (conversi) arrived at Hailes in 1246 to found a daughter house. Building operations commenced immediately on a site, where there was an ample supply of water to the southeast of the little parish church. Five and a half years later, the abbey was sufficiently far advanced for it to be dedicated. At the ceremony, on 5 November 1251, were the King, Queen Eleanor, Earl Richard, a very large company of nobles and no fewer than thirteen bishops. At this stage, it was estimated that the building operations and other expenses had already cost Earl Richard in excess of 10 000 marks. To endow the monastery, Earl Richard presented to it the church and manor of Hailes and a lump sum of 1000 marks, the latter to be spent on either building or land.

In spite of these auspicious beginnings, the community did not prosper for some time. At the time of the dedication of the church, the cloister, dorter and refectory were also complete, but building operations would not have finished then. In addition to the infirmary and other essential buildings for the monks, there were also the accommodation and granges for the lay brothers. The presence of the latter involved the duplication of many of the amenities, so adding to the initial financial burden. Ten years after the dedication of the abbey, James, Abbot of Beaulieu, visited Hailes and decreed that the number of monks and lay brothers should not be increased until the debts were diminished. In 1270, John, Abbot of Beaulieu, ordered that alms should continue to be given at the gate, this suggesting that as a matter of economy the practice had been stopped. Abbot John also had occasion to order the monks to observe the rules of silence.

In the same year, 1270, Edmund, second son of Earl Richard, presented to the community a phial of the holy blood, which he had purchased from the Count of Flanders in 1267. This bore the guarantee of the Patriarch of Jerusalem, later to be Pope Urban IV, that it was the authentic blood of Christ. On 14 September, in the presence of Edmund, the Abbots of Hailes and Winchcombe placed the phial with due ceremony in the shrine especially built for it. The possession of this was to make Hailes one of the great pilgrimage centres of England, and while in the long run this was greatly to benefit the community, its immediate effect was to put further strain on the financial resources of the house.

So distinguished a relic demanded a worthy setting and accordingly the whole east end of the church was rebuilt and extended. The form this new building took was that of a coronet of chapels radiating from an ambulatory around an apse. This design, known as chevet, had been used on the Continent for a number of years but it was to remain a rare featrue of English architecture. Beaulieu had a form of chevet dating from the early thirteenth century, but to satisfy the Cistercian demand for a simple and austere form of building the chapels were hidden behind a continuous wall and not allowed to project. At Hailes though, it was a true chevet with projecting polygonal chapels which was erected, the Cistercian Abbey of Croxden in Staffordshire probably being the model. This plan had the great advantage of not only providing a dignified area for the shrine but also for allowing ample space around it for processions and pilgrims.

The rebuilding of the church was not completed until 1277, when it was rededicated by Giffard, Bishop of Worcester. The fortunes of the community seem to have been reviving by this time for, in 1276, Hailes paid £14-13s-4d out of the "courtesy" granted to Edward I, suggesting that it was considered one of the richer houses of the Cistercian Order. Endowments continued to be made. In 1277, Earl Edmund asked the Bishop of Lincoln to appropriate to Hailes the churches of Hemel Hempstead and Northley, of which he had given the advowsons, and it seems probable that the churches of Paul and Breage in Cornwall were also a gift from him. After Earl Edmund's death in

1300 the flow of bequests slackened and the history of the next 150 years of the community is principally one of financial uncertainty. Like most Cistercian houses, Hailes relied on its flocks of sheep for the bulk of its income, wool surplus to the needs of the community being sold to the wool merchants. From this point of view, the abbey was situated in a favourable area for high-grade wool, probably obtained from Ryeland sheep. The income from this source would have fluctuated from year to year, and in addition not all the endowments were a source of profit: the Manor of Lechlade, granted by Earl Edmund at a fee farm rent of 100 marks in 1300, was such a heavy expense that it had to be given up.

In 1325, the abbot and convent sent a great petition to the Bishop of Worcester, Thomas Cobham. In it they described

TERRY BALL

Pilgrims kneel before the Shrine of the Holy Blood. The square plinth of stones remaining at the east end of the church is the base on which the shrine stood

TERRY BALL

Monks listening to a reading in the chapter house. Beyond the doorway is the cloister

their plight and indicated that the only way that they could afford to maintain the size of their community and their traditional hospitality was if they were to be granted the advowson of the church of Longborough. The bishop agreed to this request, and while the petition probably exaggerates the plight of the community, it does give an indication of the state of their affairs. In it they complain that not only were their buildings left incomplete by their founder and his son, but they had failed to obtain the promised rental of £200 a year. Many of their endowments were in distant parishes, making the collection of revenues difficult, and Lechlade, far from being an asset, was a financial liability. In the years of the great famine, from 1314 to 1321, their lands had been sterile and unproductive, and their cattle had

suffered from murrain.

A minor disaster struck the abbey in 1337 when it is recorded that at the time of vespers on the Vigil of Corpus Christi, the sluice gates of the fishponds failed. The site of these ponds can be seen to the southeast of the church. As a consequence, a quantity of mud and water flowed through the east range and into the cloister, causing much discomfort if no actual damage. In 1345 Abbot Thomas had occasion to complain that Sir Walter Dastyn and others had raided abbey property at Wormington and driven away horses, oxen, sheep and pigs valued at 100 marks, and had assaulted his men.

Hailes does not appear to have been affected by the Black Death when it first swept England in 1346-49. But the community was badly affected in

1361-62 when many of the monks and lay brothers perished. By 1386, the fortunes of the abbey were again at a low ebb. Rents were difficult to collect, the tenants and villeins were greatly reduced in numbers because of the plague, and the abbey buildings were in poor repair. To ease matters, Bishop Wakefield of Worcester appropriated to the community the church of Toddington to increase their revenues. Twenty-six years later, in 1412, Pope John XXIII, in a further effort to restore the fortunes of Hailes, allowed the Abbot to appoint suitable monks to the churches of Didbrook, Pinnock and Longbarrow in place of the secular priests, thus augmenting the community's income.

Financial troubles at this time were not entirely due to outside circumstances. In 1397 a certain Henry of Alcester was elected Abbot. In 1403, Abbot Robert of Alcester appealed to Henry IV to seize a vagrant monk, also called Henry of Alcester. This may not have been the same man who was elected abbot six years before, but Abbot Henry was certainly being blamed in 1412 for the buildings being ruinous and the community being in debt for the sum of 1000 marks. That year, the Pope, in addition to his other concessions, allowed the community to grant relaxation of eleven years and thirty-five days of penance to penitents who visited the abbey and contributed money for the maintenance of the fabric on Whit Sunday and Corpus Christi, and the seven days following each of these feasts.

At this time Hailes had a community of twenty-two monks and an income of £100 a year. It seems likely that, as with many Cistercian communities, the lay brothers had died out by the end of the fourteenth century. Certainly in the fifteenth century, the abbots were using the west or lay brothers' range for their private accommodation.

In 1431, Abbot Hendley undertook a journey to Rome to visit the Papal Curia and obtain further favours for Hailes. His mission was successful. Pope Eugenius IV granted lavish indulgences to all who worshipped God and the Precious Blood of Hailes and who gave money to the community. It is probable that from roughly this date the fortunes of the abbey revived. The discipline and financial arrangements of the house though were to come in for censure when the abbots of Beaulieu and Waverley visited Hailes in 1442. Discipline was to be tightened and the abbot was told to appoint two bursars to take charge of financial affairs. The internal and external fabric of the monastery also came in for criticism, and repairs were ordered to be made. To assist with the cost of rebuilding, indulgences were granted by Pope Calixtus III in 1458, and ten years later by Pope Paul II. To this period of rebuilding probably belong the present lavatory and part of the refectory. A little later, possibly under Abbot Whitchurch, much of the cloister was rebuilt and it seems likely that by this time the west range was fully converted for use of the abbot.

The last decades of the abbey's existence seem to have been the most prosperous in its history. Right up to the Dissolution, the "Holy Blood of Hailes" attracted the faithful. Latimer, then Vicar of Kineton, wrote in 1533: "I live within half a mile of the Fossway and you would wonder to see how they come by flocks out of the West Country to many images but chiefly to the Blood of Hailes."

The last Abbot of Hailes was Stephen Sagar who succeeded Abbot Antony in 1527. Sagar came from the Abbey of Whalley in Lancashire and appears to have enjoyed the friendship and patronage of Thomas Cromwell.

In 1538 the Commissioners were ordered to suppress all shrines and to demolish their remains. On 28 October they visited Hailes and removed the holy blood to London. On 24 November, Hilsey, Bishop of Rochester, preaching at St Paul's Cross, displayed the phial of blood and declared that it was "honey clarified and coloured with saffron, as had been evidently proved before the King and his Council."

On Christmas Eve, 1539, Abbot Sagar and twenty-one monks surrendered Hailes Abbey to Dr London and his fellow visitors. The value of the house was declared to be £357-7-8½, making it the twelfth richest Cistercian abbey in the country out of a total of seventy-five at the Dissolution, Dr London reported to Cromwell that they found "the father and all his brethren very honest and conformable persons and the house clearly out of debt." He went on to report that they had removed from the abbey "right honest sorts of jewels, plate, ornaments and money beside the garnishings of a small Shrine, wherein was reposed the counterfeit relic in times past; which all we do safely reserve unto the King's Highnes use." Abbot Sagar received a pension of £100 a year; the prior and monks amounts varying from eight pounds to one pound six shillings and eightpence.

In 1542 the Crown sold the abbey to Richard Andrews, a great dealer in monastic property, and it is likely that soon after the abbey church was demolished. The west range of the cloister, the barn and possibly other buildings, remained in repair. In the seventeenth century, the abbot's lodging with the rest of the west range formed the home of the Tracy family until they built Old Toddington House. They carried out various alterations of a domestic nature, and Kip's view (page 25) shows the house as converted by them. After the Tracys moved from Hailes, the buildings continued in use, being converted into two farm houses around 1729. A little later, the range was demolished and the building material reused elsewhere. A comparison of the Bucks' view in 1732 (page 8) with Lysons's view of 1794 (page 23) shows the extent of the demolition. The monastic barn was apparently still standing. At the end of the nineteenth century, the site was extensively excavated. Hailes Abbey was donated to the National Trust; from 1948–84 it was in the care of what is now the Department of the Environment.

The Museum

Lyons's view of the ruins in 1794, showing the remains of the west range with part of the cloister beyond

This contains a variety of exhibits on the history of Hailes, both as a monastic site and as a post-Dissolution home. Only the main exhibits are mentioned here. Of special interest are the floor tiles removed from the church, and the vaulting bosses from the chapter house and cloister. The floor tiles range from the thirteenth to the sixteenth century and some of the early inlaid tiles are of particularly high quality. The sixteen-tile Chertsey-tile on display should be noted, as should the famous Southam tile pavement. Later tiles from the site reflect the trend towards cheaper printed designs, those on display showing the loss of quality inherent in this technique. Many of the tiles carry the arms of important people associated with Hailes.

The chapter house vaulting bosses are of extremely fine workmanship, with the conventional foliage design being deeply undercut. The most remarkable of these shows Christ as a spiritual Samson rending the lion's jaw (see page 1). Six very late vaulting bosses recovered from the area of the cloister are on display. These are of significance in showing that rebuilding operations carried on at Hailes almost up to the Dissolution.

Also on view is part of a late thirteenth-century effigy of a knight, including the sword hand, portions of the forearm and three pieces of a shield, the base of which has portions of the foot of a lion of Cornwall. These were found near the junction of the south transept and the presbytery aisle. It is not certain whether they belonged to Edmund, Earl of Cornwall, who died in 1300, or to his brother Sir Richard de Cornwall, killed at Berwick in 1296.

The numerous small fragments of finely carved stone are probably from the Shrine of the Holy Blood, and from a tomb canopy.

The post-Dissolution history of Hailes is well represented by a collection of pottery, much of it of northern European origin, and some keys and clay pipes.

Some of the floor tiles from the church on display in the museum

Glossary

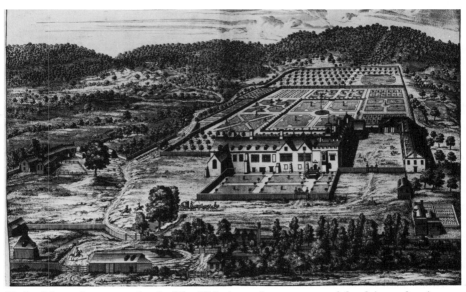

Early eighteenth-century view by Kip. This shows the west range of the cloister when it was the home of the Tracy family

Advowson   Right of presentation to a benefice

Aisle   Part of a church on either side of the nave or chancel

Ambulatory   Semicircular aisle inside east end (apse) of a church

Apse   Semicircular or polygonal east end of a church (see also Chevet)

Arcade   Line of arches

Ashlar   Squared hewn stone laid in regular courses with fine joints

Bay   Structural division of the length of a building or roof

Boss   Ornament at the intersection of the ribs of a vault or ceiling

Capital   Uppermost part of a column

Chamfer   Bevelled or mitred angle without a moulding

Chapter house   Room in which monks met daily for monastic business when an article or chapter (capitulum) of the monastic rule was read

Chevet   Polygonal apse surrounded by an ambulatory from which radiate a number of chapels (rare in English churches)

Cinquefoil   Five leaved

Cloister   Four-sided enclosure with a covered walk or alley along each side; the centre of monastic life

Corbel   Stone or wood projecton from a wall to support a weight

Day Stairs   Daytime access from the cloister to the dormitory

Dorter   Dormitory

Frater   Refectory or dining hall

Galilee   Porch extended the full width of the west end of the church, used for ceremonial purposes; porch or chapel at the entrance to a church

Garderobe   Latrine normally discharging through an outer wall into a moat or pit

Garth   Area enclosed by the cloister

Hoodmould   Weathering or dripstone to protect the head of a doorway or window

Infirmary   Hospital, sick quarters

Jamb   Side post of an opening, doorway, window or fireplace

Lancet   Narrow window with pointed head

Lavatory/lavatorium   Trough with running water where monks washed their hands before meals

Lay brothers   Monks not in holy orders who performed manual labour

Mark   Originally the value of 1 mark weight (8 ounces) of pure silver, 13s 4d (two-thirds of £1), not a coin

Mullion   Upright dividing a window or other opening into two or more lights

Nave   The part of a church extending west from the crossing

Night stairs   Stairway from the dormitory to the church for use by monks going to and from night services

Parlour   Room in which conversation was allowed

Paly   Vertical division of a shield

Pentice   Penthouse; lean-to building or covered passage or gallery

Piscina   Basin with a drain in a wall-niche near the altar for washing sacred vessels

Presbytery   Part of a church between the quire and altar reserved for clergy

Pulpitum   Screen between the nave and quire of a church, often supporting a gallery

Quire   Choir; part of a church between the presbytery and the nave

Reredorter   Building to the rear of the dorter (dormitory), containing latrines, usually flushed by a channel of running water

Retro-quire   Area behind the high altar

Reveal   Side of an opening for a window or doorway

Sedilla   Stone seats for officiating clergy built into the south wall of the chancel

Soffit   Under surface of an arch, lintel, canopy, etc

Splay   Diagonally cut-away surround of a window or doorway for increasing illumination or improving the field of view

Springer   Lowest stone of an arch or vaulting rib

Squint   Oblique opening through a wall of a church permitting a view of the altar from an aisle, side chapel or even from outside the church

Tracery   Decorative work formed by the branching of verticals (mullions) in the upper part of a window

Transept   Transverse part of a cruciform church

Undercroft   Vaulted room or cellar supporting a principal chamber above

Villein   Feudal serf

Warming house   Room in a monastery where a communal fire was kept burning during the winter